FAMILY LIFE IN
Medieval Britain

TESSA HOSKING

Wayland

FAMILY LIFE
SERIES:

Medieval Britain

Roman Britain

Saxon Britain

Second World War

Tudors & Stuarts

Victorian Britain

Series design: Pardoe Blacker Ltd
Editor: Sarah Doughty
Production controller: Carol Stevens

First published in 1994 by Wayland (Publishers) Ltd
61 Western Road, Hove, East Sussex BN3 1JD, England

© Copyright 1994 Wayland (Publishers) Ltd

British Library Cataloguing in Publication Data
Family Life in Medieval Britain – (Family Life Series)
  I.Title II.Series
  306.850941

ISBN 0 7502 1006 0

Printed and bound by Rotolito Lombarda S.p.A.

Cover pictures: (Right) A medieval marriage. (Left) Pottery jugs. (Artwork) A peasant family having lunch in the fields.

Picture acknowledgements: Ancient Art and Architecture Collection 23 (bottom); B.T Batsford 5 (bottom); British Library Reproductions 6, 7 (top); Bridgeman Art Library *front cover* (right); 5 (top), 8 (both), 9, 14, 15 (top), 18, 19 (top), 20, 25 (bottom), 26, 27 (both), 28, 29; Bodleian Library, Oxford 13 (both), 15 (bottom), 17 (bottom), 21 (top); The Master and Fellows of Corpus Christi College, Cambridge 22; C. M Dixon 25 (top); Haddon Hall 19 (bottom); Sonia Halliday 16; David MacLeod *back cover*; Museum of London *front cover* (left), 11 (bottom); National Museums of Scotland 11 (top); Wayland Picture Library 4, 17 (top), 23 (top). All artwork by Peter Dennis, except page 21 by Jenny Hughes.

CONTENTS

MEDIEVAL BRITAIN

'Medieval Britain' means England, Scotland and Wales during the Middle Ages. The Middle Ages lasted from about 1000 to 1500. The way of life changed over these 500 years, but it did so very slowly – especially for the 90 per cent of the population who were **peasants**. Only the small number of people who had wealth and power could afford to make improvements in their lives and adopt new styles.

Wealth and power came from the land. The king let large amounts of land to the Church and to great **nobles** (**barons**). Most of Britain was divided into estates called **manors**. Great nobles let some of their manors to lesser nobles (**knights**). Some land was then let in very small amounts to peasants, who in return farmed all of the land.

In both rich and poor families, land normally passed from father to son. Most landowners were men, and most heads of families were fathers. At all levels of society, however, there were women who held land in their own right and mothers who were heads of families.

This picture from a medieval book shows the three 'orders' (or levels) of society. The first shows the men and women of the Church; the second, the king and noblemen; the third, peasants and craftsmen.

We can only give a very general picture of the lives led by families in medieval Britain. At all levels of society there were wide differences of wealth and poverty. Examples have been given, where possible, from the lives of actual families. But no clear picture of family life has been left to us. Information has to be pieced together from many different sources. These sources include written records, pictures from illustrated manuscripts, carvings in wood and stone and the remains of household objects, castles and cottages.

A fourteenth-century peasant couple having trouble with their children! (From a fourteenth-century manuscript).

An amusing scene carved in wood, from a church in Gloucestershire. While a woman is busy spinning, her dog helps itself from the cooking pot.

PEASANT FAMILIES

The life of a peasant family revolved around the work of farming. Everyone who could work, took part, including the children. Home life was part of working life, and working life was part of home life. So to learn about the family life of peasants, we have to learn about the work of farming.

Peasants had to grow all the crops needed to feed their families. They also had to help farm the lord or lady's land. Children started work as soon as they were able to. We know from a law of 1388 that children learned heavy farming jobs before they were 12 years old.

PLOUGHING

Ploughing was one of the heaviest farming jobs. It was done by men in the autumn or spring, depending on the crop. These lines from the fourteenth-century poem 'Piers the Ploughman' describe a miserable scene. The family is so poor that the wife has to help her husband, and so they bring their small children with them, rather than leave them on their own.

Two men ploughing with four oxen. We can see from their expressions that it was hard work, but the men look well-dressed and the oxen well-fed. Compare this scene with the poem below.

I saw a good man hanging on to his plough.
His hood was full of holes, so his hair was sticking out.
His thick-soled shoes were so worn through
That his toes stuck out as he trod the soil.

His fingers stuck out of his two thin mittens.
He was covered in mud as he followed the plough.

The oxen he drove were so feeble-looking
You could count every rib in their sides.

His wife walked with him, carrying a long goad.
She was wrapped in a winnowing-sheet to protect her from the weather,
But she walked barefoot so the blood flowed.

A man sowing grain by sprinkling it from a hopper. Notice the birds stealing the seed.

Haymaking was done in early summer. Here two men and a woman cut the grass with scythes. In fact they are not holding them properly - the man in the middle does not even seem to be trying!

SOWING

After the cold, dark winter months, all peasants must have looked forward to spring. Nearly everyone in the family could join in with the spring sowing. Villagers set off together for one of their huge 'open' fields, where each family had a number of strips of land. The men would sow oats or barley, while the woman planted peas or beans.

Harvest time marked the end of summer. Now everyone had to join in. They had to harvest the lord or lady's crops before they could bring in their own.

KEEPING ANIMALS

Every peasant family kept animals, which supplied many of the family's simple needs. One family might own an ox, two or three cows or goats, a few sheep, pigs and chickens. The ox was a work animal. Two or three families would put their oxen together to form a team to pull farm machinery. Cows and goats were kept for their milk. Sheep were milked too, but were kept mainly for their wool. Hens laid eggs; cockerels were eaten. Pigs were the only animals kept just for their meat.

*A woman feeding chickens with her **distaff** under her arm. Peasants often had to pay their **dues** in eggs or chickens at certain times of the year.*

Tending sheep in the late Middle Ages. Some peasants owned enough sheep to sell a good deal of wool.

Peasant families lived with their animals around them. Chickens scratched for food around and inside every cottage. At night, and all day in winter, most of the animals shared the family's home. Separated only by wattle screens, they helped to keep the people warm.

Pigs were taken to grub for food in the woods. Here men are knocking acorns off the trees to feed them.

During the spring and summer, cows and sheep were taken to graze on the common or in a **fallow** field. From the age of 8, children watched to make sure they did not stray. The nursery rhyme 'Little Boy Blue', however, tells what happened if the children let their minds stray!

Little Boy Blue, come blow your horn!
The sheep are in the meadow, the cows in the corn.
Where's the little boy who looks after the sheep?
He's under the haystack, fast asleep!

During the winter, there was not enough grass or hay to feed all the animals. So each autumn all the animals not needed for work, milk or breeding were killed. The meat was then either eaten or stored, and the skins turned into leather.

9

LIFE AT HOME

A peasant family was usually made up of a mother, father and two or three children. Some had relatives living with them, and better-off families had a farm servant living in.

Very poor families lived in one-room cottages. But most lived in two or three-roomed houses built of wood, wattle and daub or stone. Every house had a garden in which vegetables, herbs and fruit were grown.

Peasant houses were not built to last long, and their furniture has not survived either. This cut-away picture has used clues from excavations to show what the inside of a family home might have looked like.

A fourteenth-century woman's hood made of wool, found in Orkney. The long fringe helped to keep the wearer warm.

An open fire burned constantly in the centre of the living room. There was no chimney – only a small hole in the roof – so the room and its simple contents became blackened with smoke. The fire was essential for cooking and warmth, but it was a danger, too. The floor was covered with straw, which easily caught fire, and the family slept on straw-filled mattresses. Babies were often accidentally burnt as their cradles stood near the fire. Pots hanging around the fire were another hazard, especially for 2 and 3 year olds. Little boys, however, died more often by falling into wells or ditches.

From 8 years old, children spent less time playing, for their parents had to teach them the jobs they would do as adults. There was much to learn. Peasant families had to make nearly everything they used, wore or ate. Boys learned to make felt and leather boots; wooden stools, bowls and spoons. Girls learned to spin, weave and make clothes; to garden, prepare food and cook.

Fragments of pottery jugs like these have been found in excavations of peasants' cottages, as well as in manor houses and towns. As they are French, they must have been bought at fairs or from travelling pot-sellers.

Pease pudding hot, pease pudding cold,
Pease pudding in the pot nine days old.

As this old rhyme suggests, peasant food was mostly plain and monotonous. The most common hot dish was pottage, a thick soup containing whatever vegetables and meat were available. Families had a simple meal such as bread, cheese and ale at midday while they were working, and pottage in the evening. A heavy type of bread was made, either in the village oven or in a pot over the fire. Women brewed ale and made different kinds of cheese. If there was anything left over they took it to a town market to sell.

In autumn, fruit and nuts were picked, eaten and stored. Meat was salted or smoked to preserve it. The family hoped that there would be enough to last through the winter, otherwise they would go hungry before spring.

Peasant families having a midday break from work in the fields. They are probably eating bread, cheese and onions - rather like today's ploughman's lunch.

A woman cooking over an open fire. Her baby seems in danger of burning its toes, while the other child keeps the fire going with the bellows.

HOLIDAYS AND FESTIVALS

Everyone went to church on Sundays and attended church festivals. On **Holy days** people were allowed off work, but the number of holidays varied from manor to manor. The longest holiday was always the Twelve Days of Christmas. At this time, there were **mummers** plays and a feast at the manor house. Summer festivals like May Day were celebrated by everyone with dancing, songs and games. Weddings and funerals saw much drinking of ale. Another special occasion was a visit to a fair, where there were entertainments, and goods on sale from other lands.

At such times peasant families did their best to forget hard work and their dues and **duties** to their lord.

Girls watching a puppet show at a fourteenth century fair. Does it remind you of a Punch and Judy show?

NOBLE FAMILIES

Unlike peasant families, noble families did not work together, nor even always live together. In return for their land, barons and knights had to fight for their king in times of war. In peacetime, too, their duties often took them away from their families. A knight, for instance, might have to guard his baron's castle, or escort prisoners to a royal court. In his absence, his lady was in charge of the manor, as well as the household which she managed all the time.

Nobles lived in households rather than families. These households were made up of family members, long-term visitors and the servants.

The largest households contained hundreds of people. With the help of her servants, the lady made sure they were all provided for.

CHILDHOOD

Children of wealthy families saw little of their parents. Babies and small children had nurses to care for them. The mother was expected to teach them their prayers, and their father to teach them to ride. They played with other children, or grown-ups, in the household.

This picture shows Sir Geoffrey Luttrell with his wife and daughter-in-law. Their family emblem covers his shield, flag and clothes.

At 7 years old, children of noble parents were often sent away to be educated in other households, which were usually grander than their own. The boys became pages, serving both ladies and knights in their new homes while they trained to become knights themselves. At first, they learned by playing fighting games with other boys their age. At 12 years old, they started to use real weapons. They had finished training by 15, and were usually knighted two years later.

Meanwhile girls were training to become ladies. By watching and helping their mothers, or the lady of their new home, they learned the many skills needed to run a household: supervising servants; storing food; making clothes; ordering supplies. They also learned fine embroidery, hunting and **hawking**, dancing, singing and how to play a stringed instrument.

Most noble children had marriages arranged for them. Parents tried to find them partners who would bring the family land. Some were even married while still children – girls at 12, boys at 14.

(Above) Noblemen and children hawking. Girls and boys learned to ride at an early age, and hunting and hawking were the favourite pastimes of noble and royal families.

Boys playing at being knights. The one on a wooden horse is tilting at a quintain (target).

MANOR HOUSES AND CASTLES

Castles were built by kings and barons to defend the countryside around them. Families who held many manors moved around, living in one after another, on the produce of their manors. Here Gerald of Wales, who was born in 1146, describes Manorbier Castle, in Wales, where he grew up.

'It is excellently well-defended by turrets and bulwarks, and is situated on the summit of a hill near the sea. Outside its walls are a fine fishpond, and a beautiful orchard enclosed on one side by a vineyard and on another by a wood of tall hazel trees. Between the castle and the church, near a very large lake and mill, a stream of never-ending water falls through a valley.'

Knights and their families lived in manor houses, which were often defended by walls or moats. Both castles and manor houses were built in many different styles. As time went on, they were made more comfortable, with more private rooms for the important members of the household.

Stokesay Castle in Shropshire, is a manor house built mainly in the thirteenth century, not by a noble family, but by a rich wool-merchant. The courtyard contained many other buildings, all surrounded by a high wall and moat.

THE INTERIOR

The main room of a castle or manor house was the hall. Here everyone ate, and some people slept. Many halls had a central hearth, but others had a fire-place at one side with a fine chimney. There was little furniture. A long wooden table was used for both eating and business.

Upstairs, at one end of the hall was the solar. This was a private bed-sitting room for the lord, lady and their small children. There was one large bed, and smaller ones which could be pushed under it during the daytime. Clothes were kept in a chest or on a pole sticking out from the wall. Tapestries on the walls, and curtains hung around the bed helped to keep out the draughts.

A man warming his feet in front of the fire in his private room in a manor house.

A lady in bed with richly decorated cover and hangings. The baby she is being handed is dressed in swaddling clothes.

When the Lady of Clare died in 1360, she left her best bedding to her daughter, Elizabeth:

'My bed of green velvet with red stripes, the coverlet of white fur and the room-hangings patterned with parrots and blue cockerels.'

Families took their furniture and furnishings with them when they moved to another house or castle. In large households, there were sometimes dormitories for groups of people like pages or the daughters of the family.

FOOD AND FEASTING

Noble families rose early, and ate a simple breakfast in private. The two main meals of the day were eaten in the hall with the rest of the household. Dinner was served mid-morning, and supper at 5 o'clock. If there were special guests, dinner or supper became a feast. A thirteenth-century encyclopedia explains that:

'At feasts...guests are seated with the lord. Children are set in their place, and servants at a table by themselves. Knives, spoons and salts are set on the board, and then bread and wine, and many different dishes. The guests are entertained with lutes and harps. At last comes fruit and spices, and when they have eaten, cloths and trestles are carried away, and guests wash and wipe their hands again. Grace is said, and guests thank the lord.'

Servants preparing dinner and taking it to table. The cook is preparing a 'cockyntrice' - halves of two different animals, sewn together, stuffed and roasted.

A lord and lady and their guests at the high table.

Many dishes were rich mixtures of meat, fruit and spices. Children were given special dishes, as red meat and fruit were not thought to be good for them. They may have been allowed this sweet cheese flan as a dessert. The recipe comes from a fourteenth-century recipe book. Can you follow it? (See page 31 for translation).

Take a croste ynch depe in trape. Take zolkes of ayren rawe and chese ruayn. Medle it and zolkes togyd and do ther-to pouder, gynger, sugar, saffron and salt. Do it in a trape, bak it and serve it forth.

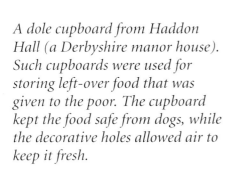

A dole cupboard from Haddon Hall (a Derbyshire manor house). Such cupboards were used for storing left-over food that was given to the poor. The cupboard kept the food safe from dogs, while the decorative holes allowed air to keep it fresh.

ROYAL FAMILIES

Royal families led similar lives to noble families, but often even more unsettled. In order to govern his kingdom, a medieval king had to travel all over it. He also travelled outside it, to defend and extend his lands.

Henry II (1133-89) of England travelled almost all the time. Sometimes his queen, Eleanor of Aquitaine, stayed in England to look after matters there, while he attended to his many lands in France. Fortunately, the king and queen had separate households. It seems that most of their children, while young, spent most of their time with their mother's household in England. The royal accounts, which can still be seen, showed what was paid for as Queen Eleanor's household moved around. For example:

1156-7 - For taking a ruska [a large wicker basket on wheels] to London for the use of the king's son...

1159-60 - For the repair of the houses and garden of the queen... and for the boy's shields.

After sixteen years of marriage, Eleanor of Aquitaine returned to her homeland of southern France, and set up her own court there. Richard, her favourite son, joined her there to complete his knight's training. Her other children also stayed at her court from time to time – all except John, the youngest,

A queen's travelling coach in the fourteenth century. Although it looks grand, riding it over bumpy roads would not have been very comfortable as it had no springs.

Royal children played with the noble children of their household. Here two boys play with shields and cudgels, while girls and boys play piggy-back.

who was put into the care of nuns as a baby. This royal family was only together at great occasions such as Christmas, when they gathered at one of King Henry's castles.

The family life of Henry III (1207-72) of England seems to have been very different. He preferred a peaceful life to military adventure. So he and his wife, Eleanor of Provence, provided a happier family life for their children, staying mainly at their castles and palaces around London. They spent a great deal of money decorating these homes and entertaining at them.

A plan of Windsor Castle as it is today. First built by William the Conqueror, the castle has been much altered and added to over the centuries, but its medieval shape is still clear. Henry II gathered his family and court there at Christmas, 1184. It was one of Henry III's favourite homes and it is still used regularly by the present Royal family.

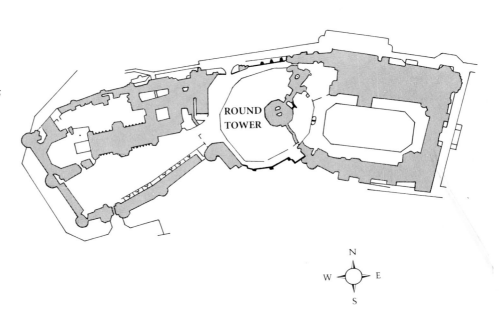

ROUND TOWER

N
W E
S

CHILD MARRIAGES

Some royal children were married while very young, because their marriages could be used to make important alliances with other countries. Here, a chronicler describes the marriage of Henry, eldest son of Henry II.

'1160 – The marriage of the king of England's son and the king of France's daughter was celebrated ...even though the boy was only 5 years old and the girl, 3.

According to the agreement between the two kings, Henry II thus gained possession of the castle of Gisors, one he had wanted for a long time.'

Unfortunately for the young Henry, he did not live to be king of England. When Alexander III of Scotland married in 1251, however, he had been king for two years – even though he was only 10 years old! His bride was Margaret, the 11-year old daughter of Henry III of England (who was Henry II's grandson). Young couples were not expected to live together as husband and wife until they were old enough. Alexander did not actually rule his kingdom until he was about 17 years old.

A fifteenth-century picture showing the coronation of Alexander III of Scotland in 1249, when he was 8 years old.

FAMILIES AND DEATH

Royal families, like all families in the Middle Ages, had to face death much more often than families do in Britain today. Their limited knowledge about hygiene and medicine meant that people died of disease, illness and infections that would now be prevented or cured.

A husband is told that his wife has just died. It was common for women to die in childbirth, or from infections shortly afterwards.

The family of Alexander III and Margaret was particularly unlucky, but the ages and causes of their deaths were not unusual. Queen Margaret died first aged 35, her youngest son died next, aged 7. The reasons for their deaths are no longer known. The royal couple's daughter died, aged 22, having just given birth to her only child. Their eldest son died on his 21st birthday, having been ill with 'a slow ague'. Finally in 1286, the king's horse tripped on a dark and stormy night and he was thrown over a cliff to his death.

The effigy of Eleanor of Aquitaine on her tomb at Fontevrault in France. Her husband Henry's tomb is on her right. Eleanor died of old age at 82, while Henry died of a sudden illness aged 59.

FAMILIES IN TOWNS

Less than a tenth of the people in medieval Britain lived in towns. Towns were smaller than they are today, and although they grew during the Middle Ages, in 1500 there were still only five towns which had more than one thousand houses.

Most towns were surrounded by walls or **stockades**, and many had grown up around a castle. Inside the walls, there were vegetable gardens and even orchards, and many families kept a few animals in their backyard. But most townspeoples' food came from the countryside. Peasants brought their produce to sell at the markets. As well as food, some of them brought the raw materials townspeople needed to buy to earn a living. Animal skins, for instance, would be bought by tanners to turn into leather, which was then bought and used by shoemakers and saddlers.

Medieval town streets were often dark, dirty, smelly and noisy.

CRAFTSPEOPLE

Many townspeople were craftsmen and women. They made goods, mainly by hand, and sold them direct to the public. Families often worked together, husband and wife teaching their children their trade. Sometimes the man carried on one trade such as glove-making, while his wife brewed ale or baked pies for sale, as well as running the home.

Their home was also their place of work. There would be a workshop in the cellar or at the back, a shop at the front, and living rooms upstairs.

Craftsmen and women often took on other people's children as **apprentices**, who lived with them a part of their household. Here is part of an apprentice's contract made in Penzance in 1459.

'John Goffe has become apprentice to John Gibbs for eight years. John Gibbs and Agnes his wife shall teach and train him in the craft of fishing the best way they know, chastising him when he needs it and providing him with food, clothes and shoes. At the end of the eight years, John Gibbs and Agnes his wife shall give John Goffe 20 shillings [one pound].'

(Above) A map of Exeter. Although this was drawn in 1587, the town still appears within its medieval walls, surrounded by the countryside. Notice the positions of the castle, gardens and cathedral.

Unravelling skeins of silk. The girl may be the woman's daughter, or an apprentice learning her trade.

The sons and daughters of craftspeople often went to school for a few years, where they learned to read and write. But it was more important for them to learn a trade, by which they would be able to earn a living. Boys, especially, were not allowed to marry until they had finished their apprenticeships – for until then, they would not be able to support a family.

Craft families who fell on hard times, widows and orphan children were often helped by their **guild**. But those without a trade could only work as labourers, and their families were often very poor.

MERCHANTS

The other main group of people in medieval towns were merchants: people who bought and sold goods – sometimes in great quantities. Some merchants became very rich – especially those who traded with other countries. The main exports from Britain were wool and woollen cloth. Most imports were luxuries, such as wine, silk and spices. Merchants sold these goods at fairs up and down the country.

*Judging from the quality of his work, this **master-craftsman** can provide well for his family. But his wife still has to spin in her spare time.*

The houses of merchants were like manor houses, with a main hall and smaller private rooms. But merchants were usually first with new ideas to make their homes grander and more comfortable – like using glass in windows. Merchants' houses built in the fifteenth century were often very decorative, their inside and outside walls, their fireplaces and furniture all carved and brightly painted.

26

A fifteenth-century jeweller's shop. The first shops as we know them appeared in the thirteenth century, when merchants sold goods they had bought, rather than made themselves.

(Right) These thirteenth-century town buildings have been reconstructed from evidence excavated at Winchester. At the front is the merchant's house, its large hall parallel to the street with two shops next to it. Behind are the kitchen, yard and outhouses, and behind them another house, yard and workshop.

Since most medieval town houses, including those of merchants, were made of wood, fire was a constant danger. But rich merchants could build their houses in the quieter parts of town, and surround them with pleasant gardens. When they became wealthy enough, merchants liked to show their importance by buying land in the country and building manor houses. Penshurst Place and Stokesay Castle (see page 16) were both built by merchants.

Pupils with their school-master or private tutor. Like most such teachers, he is a priest. Some children were sent to convents or monasteries to be educated by nuns or monks.

Men and hounds hunting a stag. Why do you think the boy is carrying a spear?

The children of merchants went to primary schools. Boys then went on to **grammar schools**. After that, some boys became merchants' apprentices for up to ten years. This meant that the sons of merchants often did not marry until they were nearly 30. Girls, meanwhile, were taught at home: how to manage a prosperous household, and how to act like a lady. They usually married in their teens.

TOWNSPEOPLE AT PLAY

A twelfth-century writer has left us a vivid description of the outdoor pastimes enjoyed by Londoners, and no doubt by people in other towns as well. For instance:

'Most of the citizens take pleasure in sporting with hawks, and in hunting in the woods where they have the rights of chase.

Children playing with a kite, whip-top and wooden push along toy.

On feast days throughout the summer the young men play at archery, running, jumping, wrestling, slinging the stone, hurling the javelin and fighting with swords. Maidens dance, and until the moon rises the earth is shaken with flying feet.

When the marsh is frozen over, swarms of young men play games on the ice. The most skilled put on ther feet the shin-bones of animals, and holding poles with their hands, they are propelled swift as a bird in flight.'

Medieval people often enjoyed watching animals fight, a sport which seems cruel to us today.

'In winter on almost every feast day, boars, armed with lightning tusks, fighting for their lives to 'save their bacon', or bulls with butting horns, do battle with the hounds let loose upon them.'

Meanwhile, young children played with toys, indoor or outdoors whenever they had the chance.

GLOSSARY

Apprentice A person learning a trade, who is bound to work for his or her employer for a set number of years in return for training.

Baron A noble who held land direct from the king.

Board A moveable table-top, set on trestles for food.

Chastise To punish, usually by beating.

Distaff A stick used to hold wool being spun into thread.

Dues Goods or money peasants had to pay their lord or lady.

Duties Work that peasants had to do for their lord or lady.

Fallow Land that has nothing growing on it, and has been left for about a year to recover its goodness.

Goad A stick used for urging animals on.

Grammar school A school where mostly Latin was taught.

Guild An association eg. of master craftsmen in a particular trade, which set and enforced regulations, and provided services for its members.

Hawking Hunting birds or small mammals with trained birds of prey (hawks).

Holy day A day on which there was a religious festival. From 'holy day', we get our word 'holiday'.

Knight A nobleman qualified in fighting on horseback.

Lady A noblewoman.

Lord A nobleman.

Lute A stringed musical instrument.

Manor An area of land usually made up of one or two villages and the land surrounding them.

Master-craftsman A qualified craftsman with his own business.

Mummer An actor in a mime play.

Noble A titled person, who held land in return for services other than farming.

Peasant A person who lived by farming the land.

Rights of chase Permission granted by a landholder to hunt on his or her land.

Stockade A very strong fence of wooden stakes.

Trade An occupation involving the making and selling of a particular type of goods. Or it can mean the buying and selling of goods.

Winnowing-sheet A strong sheet, used for tossing grain to separate it from the chaff (empty grain skins).

A TRANSLATION OF THE RECIPE ON PAGE 19.

Make a pastry case an inch [2.5 cm] deep in a dish. Take raw egg yolks and soft rich cheese. Mix them together and add powdered ginger, sugar, saffron and salt. Put the mixture into the dish, bake and serve it.

BOOKS TO READ

Davison, Brian, *Looking at a Castle* (Kingfisher Books, 1987)

Ellenby, Jean, *The Medieval Household* (Dinosaur Publications, 1984)

Macdonald, Fiona, *Everyday Life in the Middle Ages* (Macdonald Educational, 1984)

Oakes, Catherine, *Exploring the Past: The Middle Ages* (Hamlyn, 1990)

Omrod, Mark, *Life in the Middle Ages* (Wayland, 1991)

Wright, Sylvia, *The Age of Chivalry* (Kingfisher Books, 1987)

PLACES TO VISIT

Beaumaris Castle, Isle of Anglesey, Wales.
One of the magnificent castles built by Edward I of England to rule Wales.

Duart Castle, Isle of Mull, Scotland.
Isolated fourteenth century (or earlier) castle with walls over 3.5 m thick.

Haddon Hall, Bakewell, Derbyshire.
Unspoilt fourteenth century manor house. The medieval kitchens and wall paintings in the chapel are well worth seeing.

Mountfitchet Castle, Stansted, Essex.
A recreation of the wooden castle and village built on the site by one of the Norman lords who conquered England in 1066.

Stokesay Castle, Shropshire.
A smaller manor house built mainly in the thirteenth century with a typical hall and solar.

Weald and Downland Open Air Museum, Singleton, West Sussex.
Reconstructions of medieval (and later) houses including a medieval garden. Indoor displays.

INDEX